IT'S A DOG-EAT-GARBAGE WO[RLD]

REAL LIFE ADVENTURES
BY GARY WISE & LANCE ALDRICH

Andrews and McMeel
A Universal Press Syndicate Company
Kansas City

Thanks to my family for all the love, support, and material. But especially to my dad for giving me his sense of humor.

— *Lance*

I would like to thank my mom and dad for the irreplaceable gift of a wonderful childhood.

— *Gary*

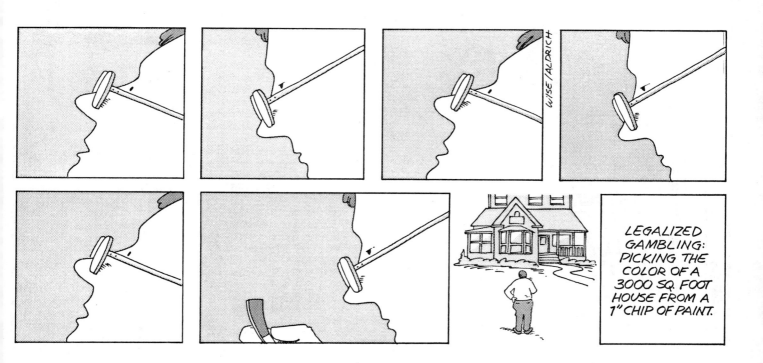

LEGALIZED GAMBLING: PICKING THE COLOR OF A 3000 SQ. FOOT HOUSE FROM A 1" CHIP OF PAINT.

5

Successful marriage tip: Never wallpaper a small room with your spouse.

Double prints: Two glossy, full-color copies of a picture that, now you see it, you really wish you hadn't taken one of.

Business Lesson No. 1: There are many things that you have no control over that you are responsible for that you know nothing about.

Thirty-two feet per second per second: No one has ever gotten on an elevator without thinking about how far they'll be going how fast if it gets loose.

Fashion hint: Don't carry everything you own in your wallet.

Man's natural herding instinct will cause the only other people in the theater to sit right in front of you.

One of those times when you wish you'd done better in math.

It's 16 feet long. It weighs 3,000 pounds. And you can't find it.

You don't know what you want, but you know you want something and you know it's in there somewhere.

Regrettably, there comes a point when one must admit to one's spouse that one is lost.

ANOTHER RELAXING AFTERNOON OF GOLFING AND FISHING.

When you go on vacation, your taste relaxes too.

Amazing fact: Although science does not yet know why, some people are invisible to waiters.

One false move on his part and the armrest is yours.

Amazing fact: As your age goes up, so does your waist.

The shame of being caught trying to pass off an expired coupon.

The quickest way to kill a plant is to buy it.

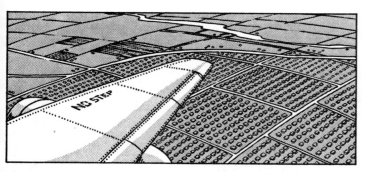

OH, WOW.

WHAT ARE YOU...
...OH, WOW.

HEY, LOOK AT THIS.

WOW.

NICE LAWN.

WISE/ALDRICH

A HOMEOWNER'S DREAM.

Calendar watches: If you don't know what month it is, how could you possibly care what time it is?

Applying little adhesive-backed flowers to your bathtub is life's only truly irreversible decision.

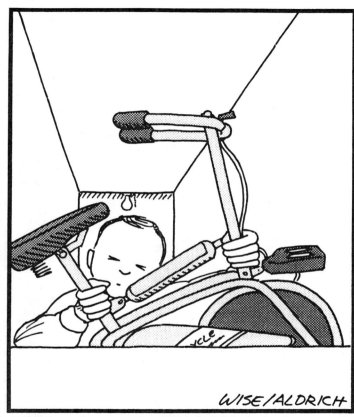

Carrying the exercise bike up from the basement and out to the garage sale will burn 170 calories.

If there is a hole in the ground, you can assume that sooner or later, there will be water in it.

Overhead projector: A visual aid that takes a dull, ponderous business meeting downhill.

Basically, the only thing that makes us superior to dogs is that we look better in sweaters than they do.

CEO/millionaire/power broker — or prom date?

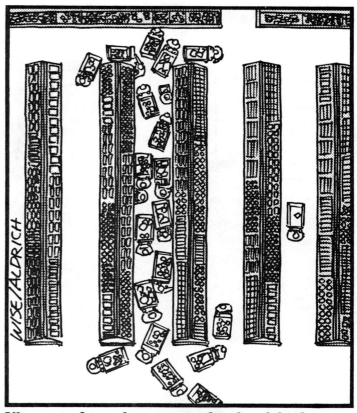

Nine out of ten shoppers prefer the aisle that you are in.

19

That little dent in your sandwich. Is it a
thumbprint or a noseprint?

So near, yet so far.

CAR.

PLANE.

SYMPHONY.

OFFICE.

DEN.

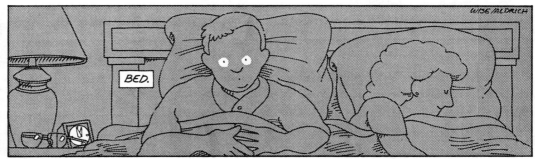

BED.

WISE/ALDRICH

"Mmnftlaptwizchrstrilkkbttzwlryqtrpdflzzurpligg . . . please pull up."

For guaranteed results, beat insect with can.

Given a choice, flies, ants, and mosquitoes prefer you.

Four people in an elevator.

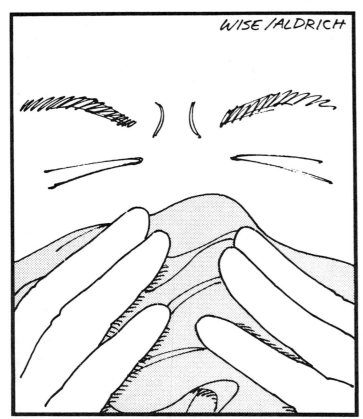

**Hankies take what you don't want in your nose
and put it in your pocket.**

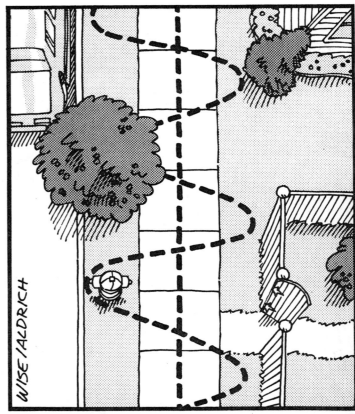

**How humans like to walk is diametrically
opposed to how dogs like to walk.**

YOUR MOM.

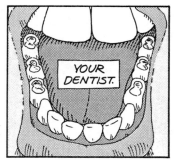

YOUR DENTIST.

YOUR KIDS WHEN THEY'RE LITTLE.

YOUR KIDS WHEN THEY'RE TEEN-AGERS.

YOUR SHOE SALESMAN.

YOUR DOG.

MUFFIN

HOW YOU'RE SEEN BY OTHERS.

It's a good thing business people don't have to hand in their meeting notes.

Never tan in the sitting position if you intend to stand up.

Fluffy decides to "just do it."

The real reason you never heard from the Publishers Clearing House Sweepstakes.

Organized people make lists but don't need them. Disorganized people make lists but can't find them.

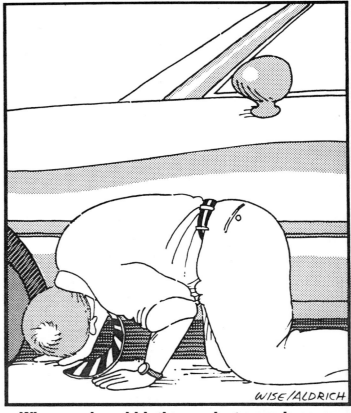

When you're a kid, the scariest sounds come from under the bed. When you're an adult, they come from under the car.

Judging by the hair in the tub, there shouldn't be any hair on your head.

A homeowner's lesson you'll need to learn but once: Just how much is five yards of topsoil?

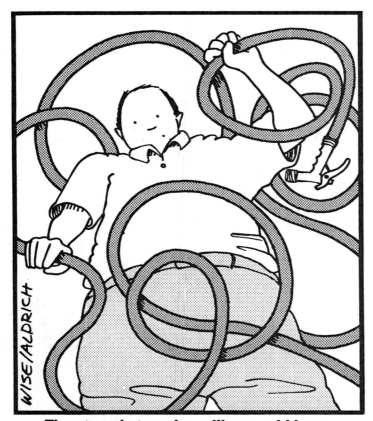

The eternal struggle: coiling a cold hose.

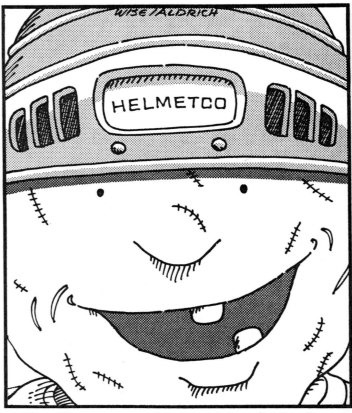

Flossing is generally no problem for hockey players.

Unfortunately, feeding children food only makes them stronger so they can throw it farther.

Monday: new challenges, new opportunities, new life-forms that grew in your coffee cup over the weekend.

Better to risk a stain than suffer the humiliation of a lobster bib.

What children see most of at Disney World.

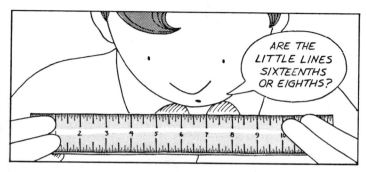

LIFE IS NEVER EASY FOR THE MATHEMATICALLY DISADVANTAGED.

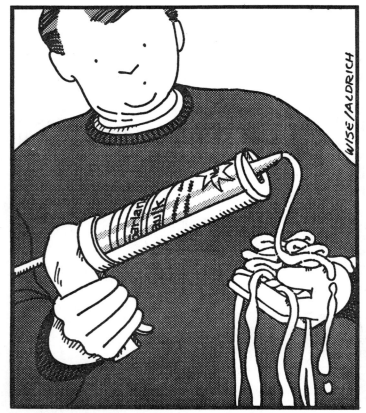

Few guns are more dangerous in the hands of the untrained.

Don't.

Looking back on your education, perhaps Ladder Safety 101 would have been more useful than Philosophy 101.

The secret guilt of skipping right to the funnies.

Standing real close to the workmen and asking a lot of questions makes you feel almost like you're doing it yourself.

Security tip: Hide valuables in the junk drawer. Thieves can't get it open either.

36

MAYBE THE REASON THEY'RE NOT BITING IS THAT IT LOOKS LIKE A RUBBER FROG WITH A HOOK IN IT TO THEM, TOO.

Company softball: an opportunity to get yelled at outside the office, too.

Why wait for the sun to burn up your lawn when you can so easily do it yourself?

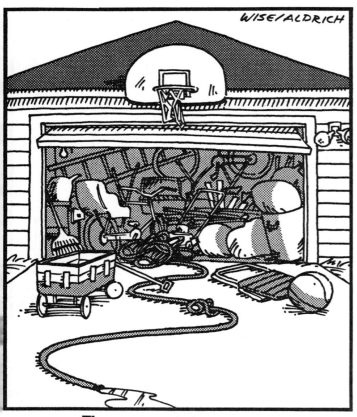

The average no-car garage.

Pasta. Possibly the world's most embarrassing food.

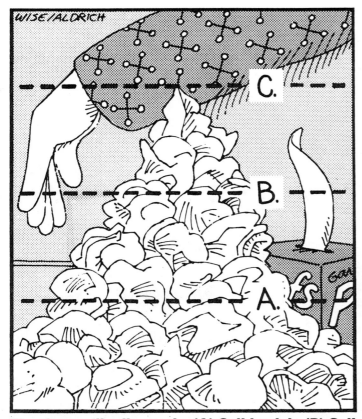

The tissue-pile diagnosis: (A) Call in sick. (B) Call a doctor. (C) Call a priest.

Getting a new power screwdriver: the insatiable need to tighten things.

Not even a multimillion-dollar contract can protect you from hat hair.

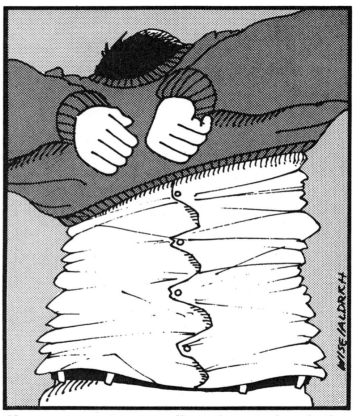

If you wear a sweater, all you have to iron is the collar.

Nothing fills those quiet moments in business meetings like stomach noises.

The ants in the cupboard aren't real thrilled to see you, either.

Chapter 4:
ROOFING FOR EVERYMAN.

Chapter 17:
INSULATE THAT CRAWLSPACE
IN NO TIME.

Chapter 8:
WIRING TIPS THAT WORK.

Chapter 32:
YOU TOO CAN PLUMB.

WHAT WOULD BE
REALLY HANDY
IS A TIP
ON HOW TO GET
YOUR HANDS AROUND
THE NECK OF THE
HOME HANDYMAN.

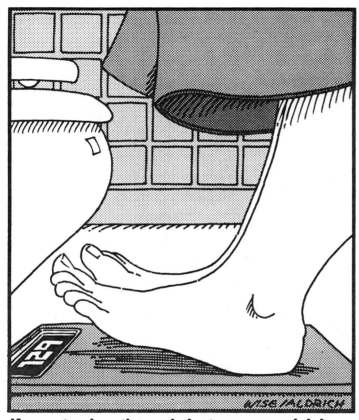

If you stand on the scale just so, you weigh less.

Either a very busy police station or a very good doughnut shop.

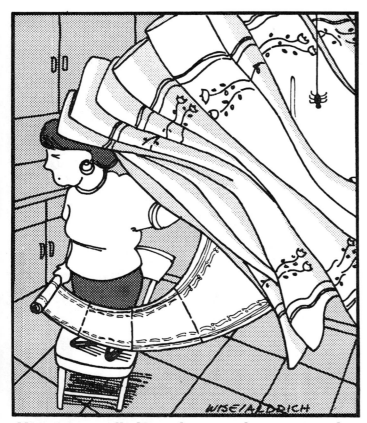

You never really know how much paper towel a spider can bite through.

Power company pruning.

An answer to the national debt. At last count, there was $69,000,000,000 caught in the couches of America.

Directions: 1. Grasp firmly. 2. Pull evenly. 3. Pick up chips.

46

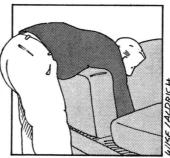

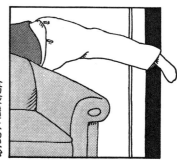

HON, HAVE YOU SEEN THE REMOTE?

THE NICE THING ABOUT A REMOTE CONTROL IS THAT IT SAVES YOU THE WORK OF GETTING UP AND CHANGING THE CHANNEL MANUALLY.

Two things children should never handle:
1. matches. 2. grape juice.

Cleaning the crisper.

What you buy just before you hire a kid to cut the lawn.

There's only one thing worse than missing the bus.

49

Amazing fact: The moment you enter a store, your memory is wiped clean of what it is you're there for.

Some people don't put up their Christmas decorations once a year. They just put them up once.

Which is really the margarine and which is really the left-over-from-Memorial-Day-potato-salad-time-bomb?

Summer is the ideal time to find those leftover Christmas tree needles.

51

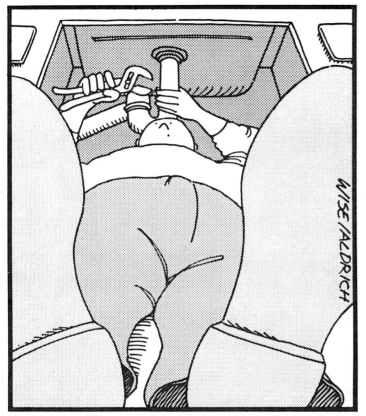

How does lefty-loosey-righty-tighty apply when you're upside down under the sink?

Seat-Bottom Cushion
May Be Used For Flotation

Good news in the event you survive the 30,000-foot fiery plunge into the ocean.

WHATEVER
YOU NEED
UPSTAIRS
IS DOWNSTAIRS.
WHATEVER
YOU NEED
DOWNSTAIRS
IS UPSTAIRS.

53

Dog bath: They end up clean and fluffy; you end up all wet and smelling like a dog.

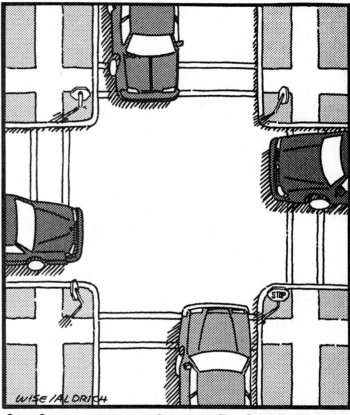

At a four-way stop, who goes first? (a) Person on right. (b) Person who got there first. (c) Person in biggest hurry. (d) All of the above.

Racing the check you wrote the day before payday to the bank.

People who worry about the rain forests vanishing need only look in your gutters.

Misery loves company and doesn't mind waking someone up to get it.

The key to business success is learning to read memos on your boss's desk upside down.

JUST HANGING UP WHEN YOU DIAL A WRONG NUMBER.

TAKING ALL THE LITTLE SHAMPOOS FROM THE HOTEL.

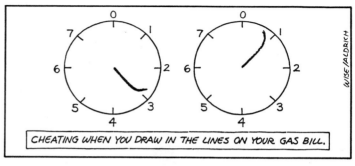

CHEATING WHEN YOU DRAW IN THE LINES ON YOUR GAS BILL.

WISE/ALDRICH

PUTTING THE OFFICE COPIER TO PERSONAL USE.

TAMPERING WITH THE LABEL ON YOUR JEANS SO NOBODY CAN READ THE WAIST SIZE.

DIRTY LITTLE SECRETS.

Now that you've put up the privacy fence you can check out the neighbors in privacy.

Every so often, the garbage disposal spirits demand a sacrificial spoon.

Lighting the gas grill.

WELL, BIG GUY...

Before ordering a vanity plate, imagine how it will sound coming from the lips of a sarcastic police officer.

Two changes that would make the race for equality a lot more equal.

Two ice-cold ice cube trays full of no ice cubes because no one ever refills them.

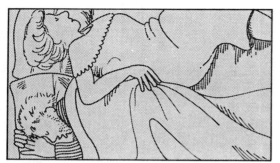

NOTHING HEATS UP THE BATTLE OF THE SEXES LIKE THE FIGHT FOR THE COVERS.

Bowls of hard candy should be changed at least once a year.

Here's hoping your hospital insurance covers more than your hospital gown does.

Unfortunately, the last thing you have to do in a public restroom is touch the same doorknob everyone else has.

Suspenders do not, in and of themselves, make you look like a CEO.

Actually, it's not a dog-eat-dog world. It's a dog-eat-chicken-bones-cereal-box-and-potato-peel world.

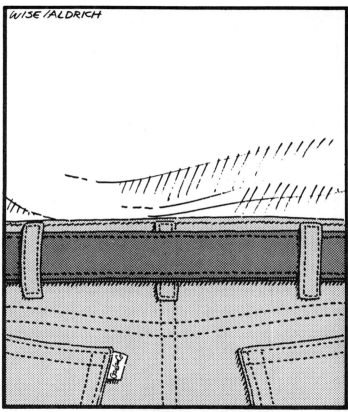

A little hint from your pants that this is not going to be your day.

64

Amazing fact: The farther you get from the ground, the more food tastes like dirt.

Today's forecast: 85 degrees and sunny. At home.

65

Packing to go on a trip.   Packing to go home.

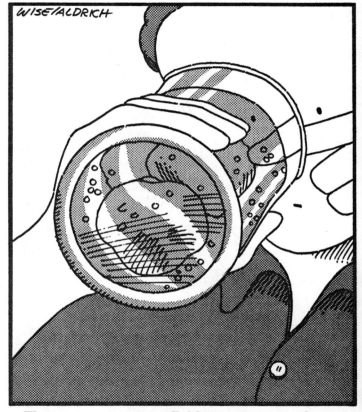

The summer games: fishing gnats out of your iced tea.

Hangers never come out alone.

No matter how hard you try, you can't remove six years of plaque the morning you go to the dentist.

Never name your pets or children anything you'd be embarrassed to yell out the back door.

331: World's record for number of times tying a tie and still not getting it right.

69

One size fits all but not real well.

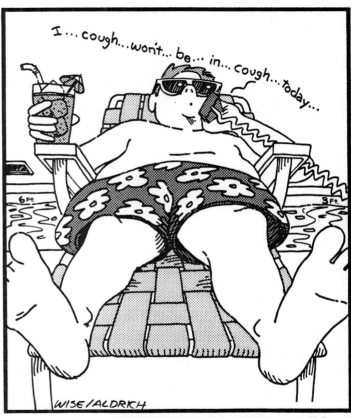

Employee tip: You sound sicker if you call in while lying down.

FIRST THING
SUNDAY MORNING.

LATE SUNDAY
MORNING.

EARLY SUNDAY
AFTERNOON.

LATE SUNDAY
AFTERNOON.

SUNDAY
EVENING.

LOOKING
FORWARD
TO MONDAY
MORNING
SUNDAY
NIGHT.

Why good dogs go bad.

**Reaching into the toilet tank: Your head knows
it's clean. Your hand isn't convinced.**

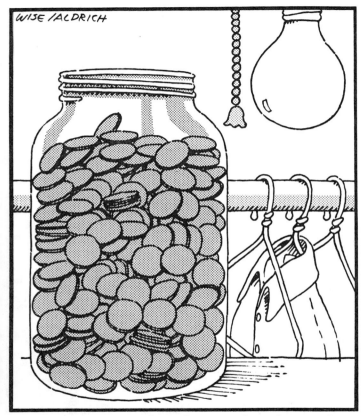

Pennies may come from heaven, but they end up in the jar in the closet.

They really are doing what you think they're doing at the other end of your speakerphone conference call.

18 feet 6 inches: The world record for hurling those annoying magazine subscription inserts that drop into your lap.

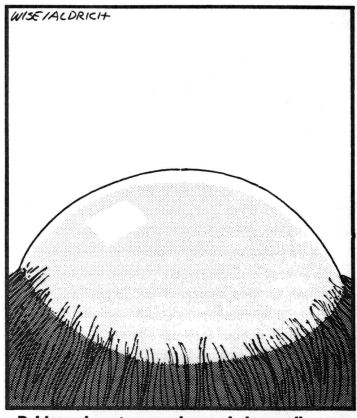

Baldness is not so much your hair receding as your skin succeeding.

74

The average fish caught on the average fishing trip averages $297.58 a pound.

The keys you can't find are under the wallet you lost right next to the cordless phone you misplaced.

75

Putting up shades is as much for your neighbor's protection as your own.

Caveman pottery.   **Adult education pottery.**

THE AVERAGE PERSON'S POSITION ON POLITICS DEPENDS ON HOW FAR BACK THE RECLINER GOES.

Group lunch economics: You ate $3, you owe $30.

Into each life a little rain must fall ... after which a lot of worms appear on the sidewalk.

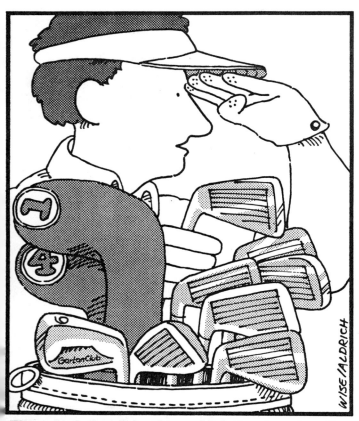

The art of club selection: carefully choosing the implement with which to send the ball screaming another 20 yards down the fairway.

A box of 100 business cards will last the average businessperson 100,000 years.

79

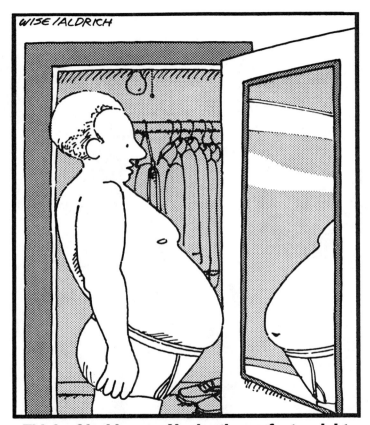

Think of it this way: You're the perfect weight for somebody else's height.

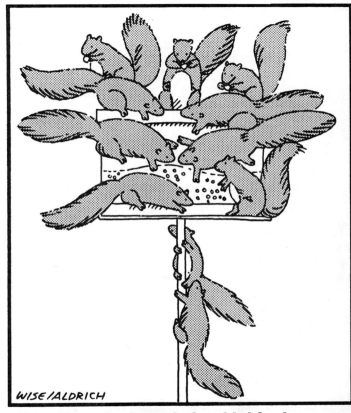

What *did* squirrels eat before bird feeders were invented?

A DOMINEERING MOTHER.

A WEAK FATHER FIGURE.

BEING THE SOLE MALE SIBLING.

LACK OF PRAISE AS A CHILD.

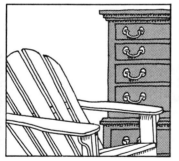

NORM, THE MASTER CARPENTER.

MAJOR CAUSES OF MALE FEELINGS OF INADEQUACY.

Hoping they won't call on you is a feeling you never outgrow.

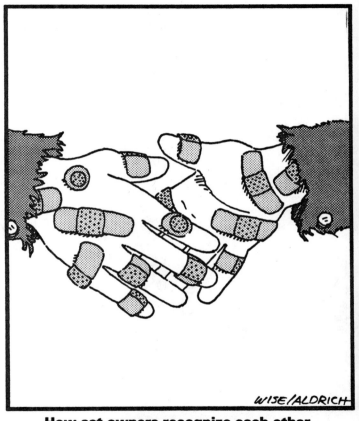

How cat owners recognize each other.

Another house brought down by the weight of one too many country decorating accessories.

A one-jar-a-week habit.

The only thing on earth that runs faster than a cheetah.

An unhealthy habit, especially if you get caught.

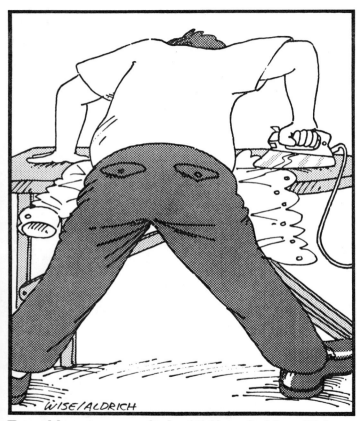

Two things men can't do: (1) Have babies. (2) Iron.

Coffee. Car. Speed bumps.

Another meeting of the men-waiting-for-the-women-at-the-mall club.

No matter how sophisticated automatic tellers look, it's hard to get over the feeling that you just stuck your money in a wall.

86

WISE/ALDRICH

THE REALLY-HOT-
PAVEMENT,
WATER-IN-THE-EAR,
SAND-IN-THE-
SWIMSUIT DANCE.

Once you've found the leg thump switch, you can't leave it alone.

Perhaps because it's so close to the brain, hair often has a mind of its own.

When people pass you, you become, for just a moment, the most interesting thing they've ever seen.

Baby on/off switch.

89

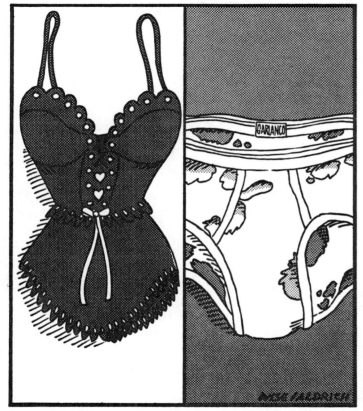

Victoria's secret. **Larry's secret.**

WISE/ALDRICH

By the time you realize you should have checked the washing instructions, they're too small to read.

WISE/ALDRICH

IF TRUTH
IN ADVERTISING
EVER HITS THE
REAL ESTATE
BUSINESS.

Most routers are sold to those with neither the capability nor the need to rout.

This . . .   is supposed to fit this?

Cheerfully filling up on 8 cents worth of breadsticks so you can't finish the $26 Scampi en Brochette.

If your lungs held as much air as your swimsuit, you could live under water.

93

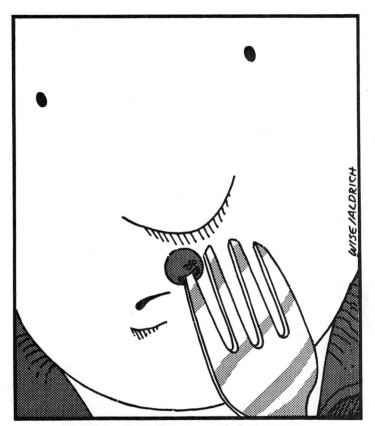

Things of no known origin: capers.

Incredibly, there is an occupation held in even greater contempt than politics.

The worst itches are always where you don't want to be seen scratching.

No decorating scheme is really complete until the toilet carpeting is in.

95

Thanks to computers, you can now lose things in a fraction of the time it used to take.

Why most dating occurs in the evening rather than the morning.

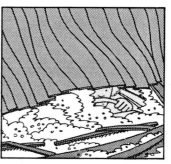

Cheating at solitaire: a victimless and, may we add, pointless crime.

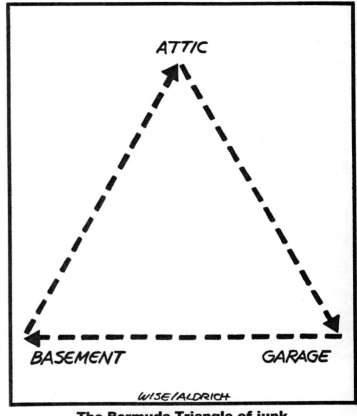

The Bermuda Triangle of junk.

Ice cream eye: an acute malady caused by eating
ice cream too fast.

Maybe the reason cigars are passed out when
babies are born is that they smell so much like
burning diapers.

99

Faulty logic of the fur-bearing.

They're called garage sales because you buy stuff in someone else's and put it in yours.

Not a good idea: 200 feet of electrical cord and a whirling blade.

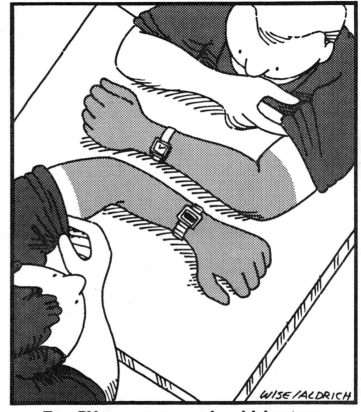

Two RV owners comparing driving tans.

Who says Americans don't read anymore?

The safety of the electromagnetic field set up by refrigerator magnets has not yet been determined.

102

One smack too many.

Cat owners are never really safe.

POT HOLES.

NAIL.

CONSTRUCTION ZONE.

WISE/ALDRICH

BIG PIECE OF TIRE.

SQUIRREL.

MRS. JOHNSON.

ROAD HAZARDS.